I0775930

Eggs and Their Uses As Food

by US Dept. of Agriculture

with an introduction by Jackson Chambers

This work contains material that was originally published in 1901.

This publication is within the Public Domain.

*This edition is reprinted for educational purposes
and in accordance with all applicable Federal Laws.*

Introduction Copyright 2017 by Jackson Chambers

COVER CREDITS

Front Cover
Telur by Hariadhi (Own work)
[CC BY-SA 3.0 (https://creativecommons.org/licenses/by-sa/3.0)],
via Wikimedia Commons

Back Cover
Cory Seward cseward15 (https://unsplash.com/photos/svazqK-ShNk)
[CC0], via Wikimedia Commons

Research / Sources
Wikimedia Commons
www.Commons.Wikimedia.org

Many thanks to all the incredible photographers, artists,
researchers, and archivists who share their great work.

PLEASE NOTE :
As with all reprinted books of this age that are intended to perfectly reproduce the original edition,
considerable pains and effort had to be undertaken to correct fading and sometimes outright damage to
existing proofs of this title. At times, this task can be quite monumental, requiring an almost total
rebuilding of some pages from digital proofs of multiple copies. Despite this, imperfections still sometimes
exist in the final proof and may detract slightly from the visual appearance of the text.

DISCLAIMER :
Due to the age of this book, some methods or practices may have been deemed unsafe or
unacceptable in the interim years. In utilizing the information herein, you do so at your
own risk. We republish antiquarian books without judgment or revisionism, solely
for their historical and cultural importance, and for educational purposes.

Self Reliance Books

Get more historic titles on animal and stock breeding, gardening and old fashioned skills by visiting us at:

http://selfreliancebooks.blogspot.com/

INTRODUCTION

It is my great pleasure to present to you another useful old book - ***Eggs and Their Uses As Food***. It was first published by the *United States Department of Agriculture* in 1901. It is also known as ***Famers' Bulletin No. 128.***

Always informative, this USDA publication delves into many facets of the humble egg. Chapters include *Uses of Eggs, Flavor of Eggs, Digestibility of Eggs, The Place of Eggs in the Diet, Marketing and Preserving Eggs, Dessicated Eggs, Egg Powders, and Egg Substitutes, Growth of the Egg Industry* and more.

A short, quick read, and as always with this USDA publications, filled with lots of useful information in a small package.

Jackson Chambers,

State of Jefferson, November 2017

Kellerstrass Farm
Arthur Oscar Schilling
1907

LETTER OF TRANSMITTAL.

U. S. DEPARTMENT OF AGRICULTURE,
OFFICE OF EXPERIMENT STATIONS,
Washington, D. C., February 15, 1901.

SIR: I have the honor to transmit herewith an article on eggs and their uses as food, prepared by C. F. Langworthy, of this Office, in accordance with instructions given by the Director of this Office.

This Department has in the past published a number of popular bulletins which summarized the available information on different food materials which enter largely into the diet of most families. The present bulletin is similar in purpose to those published earlier.

The agricultural experiment stations in a number of States have studied problems connected with the production or composition of eggs, or some other related topic, and in so far as possible the results of their work have been drawn upon.

In preparing this bulletin Dr. Langworthy has made an extended study of the literature of the subject, and has endeavored to present such data as are of general interest rather than more technical matter.

Mention should be made of the assistance rendered by Miss Elizabeth C. Sprague, late associate professor of household science at Lake Erie College, Ohio. Thanks are due Miss Sprague for the use of unpublished data and many suggestions, and also to Miss Isabel Bevier, professor of household science at the University of Illinois.

It is believed that the article is a useful summary of available information on the subject, and its publication as a Farmers' Bulletin is therefore recommended.

Respectfully,

A. C. TRUE,
Director.

Hon. JAMES WILSON,
Secretary of Agriculture.

CONTENTS.

	Page.
Introduction	5
Uses of eggs	7
Description and composition of eggs	11
Size	11
Composition	11
Composition of shell	14
Flavor of eggs	14
Digestibility of eggs	15
The place of eggs in the diet	19
Marketing and preserving eggs	23
Selling eggs by weight	28
Desiccated eggs, egg powders, and egg substitutes	29
Possible danger from eating eggs	30
Importance of the egg industry	30
Growth of the egg industry	31

EGGS AND THEIR USES AS FOOD.

INTRODUCTION.

Perhaps no article of diet of animal origin is more commonly eaten in all countries or served in a greater variety of ways than eggs. Hens' eggs are most common, although the eggs of ducks, geese, and guinea fowls are used to a greater or less extent. More rarely turkeys' eggs are eaten, but they are generally of greater value for hatching.

The eggs of some wild birds are esteemed a delicacy. Plover eggs are prized in England and Germany, while in this country the eggs of sea birds have long been gathered for food. On the eastern shore of Virginia, eggs of the laughing gull are frequently eaten, and the eggs of gulls, terns, and herons were a few years ago gathered in great quantities along the coast of Texas. Thousands of eggs of gulls and murres have been gathered annually on the Faralon Islands, off the coast of California.[1]

Other eggs besides those of birds are sometimes eaten. Turtle eggs are highly prized in most countries where they·are abundant. They were once more commonly eaten in América than now, possibly owing to the more abundant supply in former times. The eggs of the terrapin are usually served with the flesh in some of the ways of preparing it for the table. Fish eggs, especially those of the sturgeon, are eaten in large quantities, preserved with salt, under the name of caviar. Shad roe is also a familiar example of the use of fish eggs as food. Mention may also be made of the use of the eggs of alligators, lizards, serpents, and some insects by races who lack the prejudices of Western nations. However, in general, the term eggs, when used in connection with food topics, refers to the eggs of birds, usually domestic poultry, and is so used in·this bulletin.

The appearance of an egg—the shell with its lining of membrane, inclosing the white and yolk—is too familiar to need any discussion. The physiological structure of the egg is perhaps less familiar. A fertile egg contains an embryo and is at the same time a storehouse of material for the development and growth of the young individual from the embryo, until it has reached such a stage that life is possible

---

[1] The danger of exterminating these desirable birds by gathering their eggs for food has been discussed in the U. S. Dept. Agr. Yearbook, 1899, p. 270.

outside the narrow limits of the shell. The embryo is situated quite close to the yolk, which furnishes the nutritive material for its early development, the white being used later.

For convenience, birds may be divided into two groups: (1) Those in which the young are hatched full fledged and ready in a great measure to care for themselves, and (2), those in which the young are hatched unfledged and entirely dependent upon the parents for some time. Domestic poultry are familiar examples of the first group; robins and sparrows, of the second. The eggs of the two classes differ materially in composition. It seems evident that more nutritive material is needed proportionally in the first case than in the second, since the growth is continued in the egg until the bird reaches a more advanced stage of development. The quite marked differences in composition of the two sorts of eggs have been shown by chemical studies but need not be referred to further in the present discussion.

Since in all cases the egg is designed to furnish the sole source of material for growth and development of the young individual for a considerable time, it is evident that it must contain all the elements required; that is, that it must be a perfect food for the purpose intended. Milk is another familiar example of animal food containing all the elements of a complete food for the young and growing individual. Milk and eggs are frequently spoken of as perfect foods on this account. The designation is, however, misleading, for although it is true that they contain all the required elements for the growth and maintenance of the young bird or the young mammal, as the case may be, the elements are not in the right proportion for the sole nourishment of an adult individual. The food value of eggs is discussed in greater detail beyond.

Considering both wild and domestic birds, the color of the shell ranges from white through a variety of tints and mottlings. The eggs of domestic fowls are not highly colored; those of hens vary from white to a more or less brown tone, the eggs from a particular breed of hens being always of the same color. The eggs of ducks are bluish white; those of geese are commonly white; the eggs of guinea fowls are light brown, more or less mottled with a deeper shade; and the eggs of turkeys are speckled with a yellowish brown. Any special coloring of eggs of wild birds is commonly explained as a protective measure which has been developed to render the eggs inconspicuous in their normal surroundings, and therefore less easily found by their enemies. Such reasoning would indicate that the observed differences in the color of hens' eggs are due to characteristics which different breeds have inherited from remote wild ancestors. The color of the shells, whatever its reason, is a feature which has some effect on the market value of eggs of domestic poultry, though not upon their food value. (See pp. 13 and 23.)

USES OF EGGS.

The methods of serving eggs alone or in combination with other food materials are very numerous. Cooked in various ways they are a favorite animal food, taking the place of meat to a certain extent, while raw eggs, usually seasoned in some way, are by no means infrequently eaten. Boiled eggs are often used for garnishing or ornamenting different foods. Eggs are combined with other materials in various ways in many made dishes. They are used in making cakes and such foods to improve their flavor, color, and texture, while in custards, creams, etc., they thicken the material and give it the desired consistency. The white of the egg is also employed in making icings and confectionery. Well beaten or whipped egg white is used to leaven many forms of cakes and similar foods, as well as to improve the flavor. The beaten white incloses air in small bubbles, which become distributed throughout the mass of dough in mixing. The heat of cooking expands the air and makes the walls of the air bubbles firm, so that the porous structure is retained. The power to inclose and retain air when beaten varies, being greatest in the fresh egg and much lessened in packed or old eggs. Convenient leavening powders have lessened the number of eggs used for this purpose. Sponge cake, however, is a familiar example of food so leavened. This use of eggs explains some of the recipes in old cookery books which call for such large numbers of eggs. These uses are all familiar; the reasons for them are doubtless seldom thought of.

There are several simple ways of cooking eggs which are very commonly followed. Thus, the egg in the shell is cooked by immersion in hot or boiling water or is less commonly roasted. After removal from the shell, the egg is cooked in hot water or in hot fat. In the latter case it may or may not be beaten or stirred. Combined with other materials to form various made dishes, eggs are boiled, baked, steamed, or fried, as the case may be. The total number of methods of serving and preparing eggs is very large, but in nearly every case it will be found that the method of preparation is only a more or less elaborate modification of one of the simple methods of cooking.

When cooked in different ways there are marked changes in the appearance and structure of eggs. As ordinarily applied, the term "boiled eggs" refers to eggs cooked in the shell in hot, though not necessarily boiling, water. The resulting product varies greatly, according to the length of time the cooking is continued, the method of procedure, etc. Perhaps the most usual household method of "boiling eggs" is to immerse them for a longer or shorter time in boiling water. An egg placed in boiling water not over 2 minutes will have a thin coating of coagulated white next the skin, the remainder will be milky, but not solid, while the yolk, though warm, will be entirely fluid. This stage may be called "very soft boiled." If the egg is kept in boiling water 2 minutes, or a little over, the white becomes entirely coagulated. The egg thus cooked may be termed "waxy." If the boiling is extended to 3 minutes or so, the egg shows a tendency to rise in the water and will be solid throughout, i. e., "solid boiled." If the boiling is continued up to 10 minutes or longer, the "hard-boiled" egg results. The white of such an egg is hard and elastic and the yolk crumbles readily. All these changes are due principally to the more or less complete coagulation and hardening of the albumen of the egg by heat.

Numerous experiments have been made to show the changes which actually take place when egg albumen is heated. If the egg white is gently warmed no change is noticed until the temperature reaches 134° F., when coagulation begins. White fibers appear, which become more numerous, until at about 160° F. the whole mass is coagulated, the white almost opaque, yet it is tender and jelly-like. If the temperature is raised and continued to 212° F. (the temperature of boiling water), the coagulated albumen becomes much harder, and eventually more or less tough and horn-like; it also undergoes shrinkage. When the whole egg is cooked in boiling water the temperature of the interior does not immediately reach 212° F., several minutes being probably required. It has been found by experiment that the yolk of egg coagulates firmly at a lower temperature than the white.

The changes in the albumen noted above suggest the idea that it is not desirable to cook eggs in boiling water in order to secure the most satisfactory product. Those who have given attention to the science as well as the practice of cookery recommend "soft-cooked," "medium-cooked," and "hard-cooked" eggs, all of which are cooked at a temperature lower than 212° F. In soft-cooked eggs, properly prepared, the white resembles a soft, thick curd, while the yolk is fluid. Except for a suggestion of rawness, there will be little flavor, provided fresh eggs are used. Medium-cooked eggs are more thoroughly cooked than those just mentioned, the results being secured by longer cooking or by a somewhat higher temperature. The white is soft and tender and the yolk slightly thickened. The flavor (which is developed by cooking) is more pronounced than that of a soft-cooked egg and is generally considered more agreeable.

When an egg is covered with boiling water in a bain-marie or double boiler, and the temperature of the water in the outer vessel maintained at 180–190° F. for 30 to 45 minutes, the hard-cooked egg results. In this the yolk should be dry and mealy and the white solid, yet tender.

The directions given for preparing soft-cooked, medium-cooked, and hard-cooked eggs vary. The methods described in standard cookery books without doubt give the desired results if sufficient care is exercised. The chief difficulty encountered by most cooks is to secure uniform results, especially with soft-cooked and medium-cooked eggs. It must be remembered that such results can not be expected when conditions vary. The time of cooking, the amount of water used, the number, size, and freshness of the eggs, and the kinds of vessels used are important factors. Thus, eggs which have been kept in an ice chest require more heat to warm them before cooking begins than do those which have been kept at room temperature. Again, so apparently trivial a detail as the sort of vessel used (whether earthen or metal) or the place where the vessel stands during cooking may produce very different results. Many persons prefer to have eggs cooked at table in a chafing dish or other suitable vessel. In such cases the conditions may be controlled with comparative ease and uniform results obtained with a little practice if sufficient care is observed.

The following methods of preparing soft-cooked and medium-cooked eggs have been found to give uniform results in laboratory tests at the University of Illinois: Using a granite-ware stewpan of 1 quart capacity, 1 pint of water was heated over a gas flame; when the water boiled the gas was turned off and an egg which had been kept in a refrigerator was dropped into the water. Without disturbing the vessel it was covered closely and the egg allowed to remain in the water six minutes. It was then soft-cooked. As shown by tests, when the egg was dropped into the water, the temperature fell almost at once to 185° F. and then slowly to 170–171° F. If the egg remained in the water 8 minutes, it was medium-cooked. In this case the temperature of the water at the end of the cooking period had fallen to 162–164° F.

Uniform results can be obtained in the kitchen as well as in the laboratory if sufficient attention is given to details. Bearing clearly in mind the end desired, each cook must experiment for herself, as it is impossible to give directions which will apply to all cases.

The same changes which have been noted above as taking place in egg yolk and white when heat is applied in preparing boiled eggs take place when other methods of cooking are followed, though they are not always apparent.

Poached or dropped eggs are removed from the shell and then cooked in water. Thudichum recommends the use of salted water to which a very little vinegar has been added. The reason for this is perhaps that acetic acid (vinegar) tends to precipitate albumen; that is, to prevent a loss due to some of the egg being dissolved in the water. Flavor may also be one of the objects sought.

Fried eggs are generally cooked in a flat pan, in a little hot fat, oil, or butter, and may be either soft or hard, according to the length of time employed in the process. Eggs are also occasionally baked in much the same manner that they are fried.

The omelet is generally regarded as one of the most appetizing forms in which eggs can be served. It consists of the beaten egg with a little milk, water, and cream or melted butter added, quickly cooked in a little fat or butter in a suitable pan, and folded over so that it may be turned out of the pan in a half-round form. Some cooks insist that the best omelets are made by using hot water instead of milk or cream. The hot water is stirred into the egg yolk in the proportion of 1 table-spoonful to an egg. Scrambled eggs resemble an omelet in method of preparation, but no effort is made to preserve the characteristic form and appearance of the omelet. Generally speaking, lightness is desired in an omelet and thorough mixing in scrambled eggs. The former is secured by beating; the latter by stirring. Omelets are sometimes made with the addition of various materials, such as parsley, jams, etc. Many so-called omelets are made in which flour is used. These are more properly pancakes, and vary very greatly according to the ingredients used. Such dishes, as well as sweet omelets, etc., are treated of in cookery books, as are also many other ways of serving eggs which are in principle the same as those already noted, but in which the final appearance is more or less modified.

The foods in which eggs are combined with other materials range from a simple custard or cake to the most elaborate of the confection er's products. In all such dishes, as previously noted, eggs are used to give consistency, color, flavor, or lightness.

Eggs are especially rich in protein (the nitrogenous ingredient of food). This material is required by man to build and repair the tissues of the body. Some energy is also furnished by protein, but fats and carbohydrates supply the greater part of the total amount needed. Combining eggs with flour and sugar (carbohydrates) and butter, cream, etc. (fat), is perhaps an unconscious effort to prepare a food which shall more nearly meet the requirements of the body than either ingredient alone. When eggs, meat, fish, cheese, or other similar foods rich in protein are eaten, such other foods as bread, butter, potatoes, etc., are usually served at the same time, the object being, even if the fact is not realized, to combine the different classes of nutrients into a suitable diet. The wisdom of such combination, as well as of other generally accepted food habits, was proved long ago by practical experience. The reason has been more slowly learned.

As previously stated, egg white when heated at the temperature of boiling water for a considerable time becomes hard and contracts. This explains the curdling of custards, shrinkage and toughening of omelets, souffles, meringues, sponge cake, and similar mixtures. The firm coagulation of albumen at 212° F. explains the use of egg white for clarifying coffee, soup, or other liquids. The albumen, which is mixed with the liquid before boiling, coagulates and incloses the floating particles, leaving the liquor clear. When eggs are removed from the shell a little of the white usually clings to the inner surface unless it is scraped. Such eggshells are often used for clarifying purposes instead of the whole egg. The clarifying properties are, of course, due to the egg white and not to the shells.

The uses of eggs for other purposes than food are numerous. Large quantities of egg white are used in the manufacture of albumen paper for photographic purposes, and the egg white and yolk, and products made from them, are very important in the manufacture of many different articles.

DESCRIPTION AND COMPOSITION OF EGGS.

Size.—The eggs of different kinds of domestic poultry vary in size as well as appearance, and there is also a considerable range in the size of eggs of different breeds; thus, hens' eggs range from the small ones laid by bantams to the large ones laid by such breeds as Light Brahmas. On an average, a hen's egg is 2.27 inches in length and 1.72 inches in diameter or width at the broadest point, and weighs about 2 ounces, or 8 eggs to the pound (1½ pounds per dozen). Generally speaking, the eggs of pullets are smaller than those of old hens, those of ducks somewhat larger than hens' eggs, while those of turkeys and geese are considerably larger. Guinea eggs, on an average, measure 1½ by 1½ inches, are rather pointed at one end, and weigh about 1.4 ounces each, or 17 ounces to the dozen. Goose eggs weigh about 5.5 to 6.7 ounces each, or about 5 pounds to the dozen—that is, more than three times as much as hens' eggs. The eggs of wild birds are said to be smaller than those of the same species when domesticated. Wild ducks' eggs are said to be, on an average, 1.97 to 2.17 inches in diameter, domestic ducks' eggs 2.36 to 2.56 inches.

Composition.—The shells of hens' eggs constitute about 11 per cent, the yolk 32 per cent, and the white 57 per cent of the total weight of the egg. According to tests made at the New York State Experiment Station, white-shelled eggs have a somewhat heavier shell than brown-shelled eggs. The shell of a duck's egg constitutes about 14 per cent of the total weight, and that of a plover egg 10 per cent. The following table shows the composition of hens' eggs, raw and cooked, brown-shelled and white-shelled, and of egg white and yolk, as well as the composition of the egg (whole egg white and yolk) of the guinea fowl, duck, goose, turkey, and plover, also evaporated eggs and egg substitutes. For purpose of comparison, the composition of beefsteak and several other familiar animal foods, and of wheat flour and potatoes, is also added.

Average composition of eggs, egg products, and certain other foods.

	Refuse.	Water.	Protein.	Fat.	Carbo-hydrates.	Ash.	Fuel value per pound.
	Per cent.	Per cent.	Per cent.	Per cent.	Per cent.	Per cent.	Calories.
Hen:							
Whole egg as purchased...	11.2	65.5	11.9	9.3	....	0.9	635
Whole egg, edible portion .	....	73.7	13.4	10.5	....	1.0	720
White	....	86.2	12.3	.2	....	.6	250
Yolk	....	49.5	15.7	33.3	....	1.1	1,705
Whole egg boiled, edible portion	....	73.3	13.2	12.0	....	.8	765
White-shelled eggs as purchased	10.7	65.6	11.8	10.8	....	.6	675
Brown-shelled eggs as purchased..................	10.9	64.8	11.9	11.2	....	.7	695
Duck:							
Whole egg as purchased...	13.7	60.8	12.1	12.5	....	.8	750
Whole egg, edible portion .	....	70.5	13.3	14.5	....	1.0	860
White	....	87.0	11.1	.03	....	.8	210
Yolk	....	45.8	16.8	36.2	....	1.2	1,840
Goose:							
Whole egg as purchased...	14.2	59.7	12.9	12.3	....	.9	760
Whole egg, edible portion .	....	69.5	13.8	14.4	....	1.0	865
White	....	86.3	11.6	.02	....	.8	215
Yolk	....	44.1	17.3	36.2	....	1.3	1,850
Turkey:							
Whole egg as purchased...	13.8	63.5	12.2	9.7	....	.8	635
Whole egg, edible portion .	....	73.7	13.4	11.2	....	.9	720
White	....	86.7	11.5	.03	....	.8	215
Yolk	....	48.3	17.4	32.9	....	1.2	1,710
Guinea fowl:							
Whole egg as purchased...	16.9	60.5	11.9	9.9	....	.8	640
Whole egg, edible portion .	....	72.8	13.5	12.0	....	.9	755
White	....	86.6	11.6	.03	....	.8	215
Yolk	....	49.7	16.7	31.8	....	1.2	1,655
Plover:							
Whole egg as purchased a .	9.6	67.3	9.7	10.6	....	.9	625
Whole egg, edible portion a	....	74.4	10.7	11.7	....	1.0	695
Evaporated hens' eggs	....	6.4	46.9	36.0	7.1	3.6	2,525
Egg substitute...............	....	11.4	73.9	.3	5.3	9.1	1,480
Pudding (custard) powder a ..	....	13.0	2.1	3.4	80.9	.6	1,690
Cheese as purchased	....	34.2	25.9	33.7	2.4	3.8	1,950
Sirloin steak as purchased	12.8	54.0	16.5	16.1	....	.9	985
Sirloin steak, edible portion...	....	61.9	18.9	18.5	....	1.0	1,130
Milk......................	....	87.0	3.3	4.0	5.0	.7	325
Oysters in shell as purchased..	81.4	16.1	1.2	.2	.7	.4	45
Oysters, edible portion	....	86.9	6.2	1.2	3.7	2.0	235
Wheat flour	....	12.0	11.4	1.0	75.1	.5	1,650
Potatoes as purchased.........	20.0	62.6	1.8	.1	14.7	.8	310
Potatoes, edible portion	....	78.3	2.2	.1	18.4	1.0	385

a European analyses.

The above figures represent average values. Individual specimens vary more or less from the average.

As is shown by analysis, eggs consist chiefly of two nutrients—protein and fat—in addition to water and mineral matter or ash. Carbohydrates are present in such small amounts that they are usually neglected in the analysis. The protein or nitrogenous matter is the nutrient which is needed to build and repair body tissue, as already stated, while the fat is useful for supplying energy. Some energy is also derived from protein. Mineral matter is required by the body for many purposes, but less is definitely known concerning the kind and amount required than in the case of the other constituents.

In composition, eggs of all sorts resemble such animal foods as meat, milk, and cheese, more than such vegetable foods as flour and potatoes. As will be seen by the figures in the above table, hens' eggs and those of other domestic fowls do not differ greatly in composition. Neither does the cooked egg vary materially in composition from the raw, though it varies markedly in texture. The yolk and white differ greatly in composition. The yolk contains considerable fat and ash, while the white is practically free from fat and has a very small ash content. The white contains somewhat less protein and about half as much water as the yolk. As is usually the case with our familiar foods, the water is not visible as such, but is combined or mingled with the other constituents, so that the whole food is more or less moist, liquid or juicy.

The figures quoted in the table show that there is practically no difference in composition between hens' eggs with dark shells and those with white shells, although there is a popular belief that the former are "richer." This point was studied by the New York State and California Experiment Stations, many analyses of the two sorts of eggs being made. At the California Experiment Station the brown-shelled eggs were laid by Partridge Cochins, Dark Brahmas, Black Langshans, Wyandottes, and Barred Plymouth Rocks. The white-shelled eggs were laid by Brown Leghorns and Buff Leghorns, White Minorcas and Black Minorcas. The Michigan Experiment Station also analyzed the eggs of a number of different breeds, though the special object was not to determine whether there was any relation between the color of the shell and the composition of the eggs. However, no constant variation in the eggs of the different breeds was observed. These tests and others like them justify the statement that the eggs of one breed, whatever the color of the shells, are as nutritious as those of another, provided they are of the same size and the fowls are equally well fed.

As shown by their composition, eggs are nutritious food. They are less concentrated—i. e., contain more water—than cheese, but are more concentrated than milk or oysters. In water content they do not differ greatly from the average value for lean meat. The kinds and amounts of nutrients in eggs indicate that they may be properly used in the diet in the same way as most other animal foods, and this belief is confirmed by the experience of uncounted generations.

The table shows the nutrients in different kinds of eggs and in a few other foods. Many studies have been made of the chemical bodies making up the different classes of nutrients. Egg white is sometimes said to be pure albumen. In reality it consists of several albumens, and, according to many observers, a little carbohydrate material. The phosphorus in the albumen of the egg white is equivalent to about 0.03 per cent phosphoric acid. The chief ash constituent is sodium chlorid (common salt).

A very extended investigation of the white of egg was made at the Connecticut State Experiment Station. The "albumen" or protein of egg white was found to consist of four bodies—ovalbumen, conalbumen, ovomucin and ovomucoid. The ovalbumen is the chief constituent and makes up the greater part of the egg white. The conalbumen has much the same chemical properties as ovalbumen. Ovomucin and ovomucoid are glycoproteids, and are present in small amounts.

Egg yolk contains a number of different bodies, including about 15 per cent vitellin (a proteid); 20 per cent palmatin, stearin, and olein (the fatty constituents), and 0.5 per cent coloring matter, besides small amounts of lecithin (a fat-like body containing phosphorus), nuclein, etc. The total phosphorus in the yolk is equivalent to a little over 1 per cent of phosphoric acid. Besides phosphorus, the yolk contains such chemical elements as calcium, magnesium, potassium, and iron in the form of salts and other chemical compounds. The protein of egg yolk was studied extensively at the Connecticut State Experiment Station. According to these investigations it contains a large amount of proteid matter combined with lecithin. The name lecithin-nucleo-vitellin is proposed for this compound, which behaves like a globulin. It is soluble in a solution of salt. As prepared in the laboratory the lecithin-nucleo-vitellin contained from 15 to 30 per cent lecithin. A lecithin-free body insoluble in salt solution was also isolated. This was called nucleo-vitellin.

One of the constituents of egg albumen is sulphur. The dark stain made by eggs on silver is commonly and doubtless correctly attributed to the formation of silver sulphid. The albumens are readily decomposed with the liberation of hydrogen sulphid. The bad odor of rotten eggs is due largely to the presence of this gas and phosphureted hydrogen, which is also formed. The shell of the egg is porous, and the micro-organisms which cause the egg to ferment—i. e., to rot or spoil—gain access to the egg through the minute openings. Like the mold spores, these micro-organisms are widely distributed.

Composition of shell.—In the table no figures are given for the composition of the eggshell, which, of course, has no food value. The shell of the hen's egg is made up very largely of mineral matter, containing 93.7 per cent calcium carbonate, 1.3 per cent magnesium carbonate, 0.8 per cent calcium phosphate, and 4.2 per cent of organic matter. The shells of goose eggs, on an average, have the following percentage composition: Calcium carbonate, 95.3; magnesium carbonate, 0.7; calcium phosphate, 0.5, and organic matter, 3.5. The shells of ducks' eggs contain 94.4 per cent calcium carbonate, 0.5 per cent magnesium carbonate, 0.8 per cent calcium phosphate, and 4.3 per cent organic matter. The shells of other eggs are doubtless of much the same composition.

FLAVOR OF EGGS.

It is generally conceded that eggs which are perfectly fresh have the finest flavor. After eggs have been kept for a time the flavor deteriorates, even if there is no indication of spoiling. Such differences are especially important when eggs are used for table purposes. Stale eggs are not regarded as palatable, and the flavor of spoiled eggs is such that for this, if for no other reason, they are totally unfit for food. The flavor of even perfectly fresh eggs is not always satisfactory, since it is influenced more or less by the character of the food eaten by the laying hens. The New York State Experiment Station studied the effect of different rations upon the flavor of eggs. Those laid by hens fed a highly nitrogenous ration were inferior to those from hens fed a carbonaceous ration. They had a disagreeable flavor and odor, the eggs and yolk were smaller, and the keeping qualities were inferior. In a test at the Massachusetts (Hatch) Experiment Station to compare cabbage and clover rowen as the green portion of a ration for laying hens, it was found that the eggs produced on the former ration, although heavier and possessing a higher percentage of dry matter, protein, and fat, were inferior in flavor and cooking qualities to eggs produced on the ration containing clover. The North Carolina Experiment Station studied the effect of highly flavored food upon the eggs produced. A small quantity of chopped wild onion tops and bulbs was added to the feed of a number of hens. After about two weeks the onion flavor was noticed in the eggs laid. When the amount of onion feed was increased the flavor became so pronounced that the eggs could not be used. A week after the feeding of onions was discontinued the disagreeable flavor was no longer noticed. From these tests it appears that the flavor of eggs may be materially influenced by the food consumed. This is a matter of importance, especially when poultry are kept to supply eggs for table use.

DIGESTIBILITY OF EGGS.

Raw eggs or eggs only slightly cooked are commonly said to be very digestible, the idea being obviously that they digest readily without giving rise to pain or other physical discomfort. The term digestibility has another meaning and one which is commonly intended when it is used in the discussion of food values. This refers to the thoroughness of digestion, that is, to the total amount of material which any food gives up to the body in its passage through the digestive tract. Since only soluble or possibly emulsified matter can pass through the walls of the stomach and intestines and be taken up into the circulation to nourish the body, it follows that only material which is soluble or is rendered soluble by the action of pepsin, trypsin, and other ferments in the digestive juices, is truly digestible. The original condition of food, the method of cooking, and the amount eaten at a given time, are among the factors which determine the quantity of any given material which can be digested.

Statements are frequently made with regard to the length of time required to digest different foods. Many of these are doubtless far from accurate, as the subject is not easy to study. By methods of artificial digestion the length of time required to render different foods soluble has been frequently tested. It is possible to use in the experiments the same digestive ferments which occur in the body and to approximate body temperature, etc., but it is quite certain that all the conditions of digestibility in the body can not be reproduced in the laboratory. The results obtained are interesting and often valuable, but it is worthy of note that careful investigators are much slower to make sweeping deductions from them than are popular writers on the subject.

Some years ago Dr. Beaumont, a United States Army surgeon, had an excellent opportunity for studying digestibility in the stomach. A healthy young man was accidentally wounded in the stomach by the discharge of a musket. In time the large wound inflicted healed, leaving a permanent opening into the stomach, which was ordinarily closed by a valvular flap made by a fold of the stomach lining, which could be easily pushed aside and the interior of the stomach examined or the stomach contents removed as desired. Strange as it may seem, this could be done without giving the subject pain or annoyance, nor was his general health abnormal after the wound had healed in this curious way. For many years after the time of the accident (1822) the man was under Dr. Beaumont's care and observation. Very many experiments were made on the length of time required by different foods for digestion in the stomach, or "chymification." Many artificial digestion experiments were also made, using gastric juice removed from the man's stomach. Although these investigations were carried on long before the theories and methods of physiological chemistry now accepted were known, so much care was taken in making the experiments, and in recording the experimental data, that the work has never ceased to be of great value as well as interest. However, it should not be forgotten that Dr. Beaumont studied only digestion in the stomach; his work throws no light on digestion in the intestines. This is of especial importance in the case of starchy foods, as the digestion of starch, which is begun by the saliva, ceases in the stomach but is resumed in the intestines. The experiments reported include tests of the length of time required to digest eggs, hard and soft boiled, fried, roasted, and raw. The raw eggs were sometimes whipped and sometimes not. In all the tests fresh eggs were used. Hard boiled and fried eggs each required $3\frac{1}{2}$ hours for digestion in the stomach, i. e., for the formation of chyme; soft boiled eggs required 3 hours; roasted eggs, $2\frac{1}{4}$ hours; raw eggs, not whipped, 2 hours; and raw eggs, whipped, $1\frac{1}{2}$ hours. When tested by the methods of artificial digestion followed by Dr. Beaumont, which approximate bodily conditions as closely as he was able to make them, the hard boiled eggs required 8 hours for digestion; soft boiled eggs, $6\frac{1}{2}$ hours; raw eggs, not whipped, $4\frac{1}{2}$ hours; and raw eggs, whipped, 4 hours. The two methods gave results which agree in the relative length of time required for the digestibility of the different samples, though not in the actual time required. Similar results were obtained by the two methods with the greater part of the large number of foods studied. One of Dr. Beaumont's general deductions was that most of the common foods required from 2 to 4 hours to digest in the stomach. He says further:

The time required for the digestion of food is various, depending upon the quantity and quality of the food, state of the stomach, etc., but the time ordinarily required for the disposal of a moderate meal of the fibrous parts of meat, with bread, etc., is from 3 to $3\frac{1}{2}$ hours.

As regards the time required for digestion in the stomach it will be seen that in this investigation eggs compare favorably with other common foods. It must be remembered that digestion continues in the intestine, and that no data are furnished by these experiments for judging of this factor. This is an important matter, as food material which escapes digestion in the stomach may be thoroughly digested later in the intestine. This fact seems to have been often overlooked in the discussion of Dr. Beaumont's work.

Among later experiments on the digestibility of eggs by artificial methods, the work of the Minnesota Experiment Station may be cited. The object was to study the thoroughness as well as the ease of digestion. Five experiments were made by means of a pepsin solution with eggs cooked under different conditions. Eggs were cooked for 3 minutes in water at 212° F., giving a "soft-boiled" egg, and for 5 minutes and 20 minutes at the same temperature. The egg boiled 3 minutes and digested for 5 hours in pepsin solution, compared with one boiled 20 minutes and treated in the same way, showed 8.3 per cent undigested protein in the former, against 4.1 per cent undigested protein in the latter. Under similar treatment the egg boiled 5 minutes gave 3.9 per cent undigested protein. In all cases the egg was quite thoroughly digested. Another trial was then made in which the eggs were cooked for periods of 5 and 10 minutes in water at 180° F.—that is, the albumen was coagulated at a lower temperature than that of boiling water. In both of these cases the protein was entirely digested in 5 hours. These results would indicate that while the time and the temperature of cooking has some effect upon the rate of digestion, it does not very materially affect the total digestibility.

As regards the general deduction that eggs cooked for different lengths of time vary somewhat in the length of time for digestion under the experimental conditions, the results agree quite closely with those obtained by Dr. Beaumont.

Experiments have also been made with man to learn how thoroughly eggs are digested. In such tests it is usual to analyze the food and the feces, the latter being assumed to consist principally of undigested food. Deducting the amount of the different nutrients in the feces from the total amount consumed, shows how much of each nutrient was digested. Such an experiment was made at the Minnesota Experiment Station with a healthy man. A very considerable portion of the nitrogenous material and fat of the ration was furnished by eggs, the other foods eaten being potatoes, milk, and cream. About 90 per cent of the total nitrogenous material and over 90 per cent of the fat consumed were digested. In experiments at the University of Tennessee with healthy men on a diet of bread, milk, and eggs, from 93 to 95 per cent of both the protein and fat were digested. The conclusion therefore seems warranted that, as shown by composition and digestibility, eggs possess the high nutritive properties which are popularly assigned to them.

A German investigator, Rubner, some years ago tested the digestibility of hard-boiled eggs with a healthy man. No other food was eaten with the eggs. It was found that 95 per cent of the total dry matter and 97 per cent of the protein were digested. The fat was also very thoroughly assimilated. The percentage of total dry matter and protein digested was about the same as Rubner found in similar experiments in which. meat only was eaten, while the percentage of fat digested was larger. Discussing these tests, Rubner says in effect:

From the fact that eggs are as completely digested as meat, it does not follow that they are digested in the same time, or that hard-boiled eggs do not produce more disturbance in the.digestive organs. It is highly probable that there is no difference in the thoroughness of digestion of hard-boiled and soft-boiled eggs.

Jorissenne, discussing the disgestibility of eggs with reference to some recent European work on the subject, states that he regards the yolk of raw, soft-boiled, and hard-boiled eggs as equally digestible. The white of soft-boiled eggs being semiliquid, offers little more resistance to the digestive juices than raw white. The white of a hard-boiled egg is not generally very thoroughly masticated. Unless finely divided, it offers more resistance to the digestive juices than the fluid or semifluid white, and undigested particles may remain in the digestive tract many days and decompose. From this deduction it is obvious that thorough mastication is a matter of importance. Provided mastication is thorough, marked differences in the completeness of digestion of the three sorts of eggs, in the opinion of the writer cited, will not be found.

Perhaps the most extended study of the digestibility of eggs was carried on recently at St. Petersburg, by Tikhvinski. Two experiments, each divided into two periods of seven days, were made with a healthy man. In the first period of the first experiment, the diet consisted of hard-boiled eggs, bread, and meat; in the second, of soft-boiled eggs with bread and meat. The second experiment was made under similar conditions, except that the soft-boiled eggs were used in the first period and the hard-boiled in the second. The eggs furnished about one-fifth of the total protein and two-thirds of the total fat of the diet. Considering the average results of the whole investigation or those of each experiment, the rations containing the eggs cooked in the two ways proved equally digestible, 90 to 91 per cent of the protein and 95 per cent of the fat consumed being retained in the body. As the only factor in the experiments which varied was the time of cooking the eggs, the deduction seems warranted that the hard and soft boiled were equally digestible.

From experimental evidence it seems fair to conclude that eggs are quite thoroughly digested and that the length of time of cooking has less effect upon this factor than upon the time required for digestion. In a healthy man the latter consideration is probably not a matter of much importance. In the diet of sick persons and invalids it may be more important. Diet in such cases, however, is a matter for the attention of skilled physicians.

In some of the experiments referred to above the eggs were used alone; in others, as a part of a more or less simple mixed diet. The effect of one food upon the digestibility of another is a matter concerning which little is definitely known. It is possible that when two foods are eaten together, the digestibility of either or both is (1) unchanged, (2) increased, or (3) diminished.

Apparently no experiments have been made in which the problem was studied with special reference to eggs combined with other foods. However, artificial digestion experiments were made by Fraser on the effect of beverages on the digestibility of a number of foods including raw and cooked egg albumen, which led to the deduction that tea, coffee, and cocoa retarded somewhat the digestibility of the nitrogenous constituents of eggs, although the effect was less marked with coffee than with the other beverages. Water did not have this effect.

Though interesting in themselves, too wide application should not be made of the results of such tests, for even if the beverages retarded digestibility somewhat, it does not necessarily follow that this effect was harmful, or that the thoroughness of digestion was altered.

THE PLACE OF EGGS IN THE DIET.

Eggs are used in nearly every household in some form or another in varying amounts. From the results of the numerous dietary studies, made under the auspices of this Department and by the agricultural experiment stations, it has been calculated that on an average eggs furnish 3 per cent of the total food, 5.9 per cent of the total protein, and 4.3 per cent of the total fat used per man per day. Cheese was found to furnish 0.4 per cent of the total food, 1.6 per cent of the total protein, and 1.6 per cent of the total fat, while the milk and cream together furnish 19.9 per cent of the total food, 10.5 per cent of the total protein, and 10.7 per cent of the total fat. Milk and cream together also furnish some carbohydrates, while eggs and cheese furnish no appreciable amount of this group of nutrients. Considering some of the common meats, beef and veal together were found to furnish 10.3 per cent of the total food, 24.6 per cent of the total protein, and 19.5 per cent of the total fat. The corresponding values for mutton and lamb together were 1.4, 3.3, and 3.8 per cent.

It will be seen that, judged by available statistics, eggs compared favorably with the more common animal foods, as regards both the total food material and the total protein and fat furnished by them in the average daily dietary. In other words, investigations show that the high food value of eggs is appreciated and that they constitute one of the very important articles of diet in the American household.

The amount of nutritive material which a given amount of eggs will furnish at any stated price per dozen may be readily calculated. When eggs are 15 cents per dozen, 10 cents expended for this food will furnish 1 pound total food material, containing 0.13 pound protein and 0.09 pound fat, the whole having a fuel value of 635 calories. At 25 cents per dozen, 10 cents worth of eggs will furnish 0.60 pound total food material, supplying 0.08 pound of protein, 0.05 pound of fat, and 380 calories. At 35 cents per dozen, 10 cents will procure 0.43 pound total food material containing 0.06 pound of protein, 0.04 pound of fat, and furnish 275 calories. Ten cents expended for beef at 8 cents per pound will furnish 1.25 pounds total food material, containing 0.24 pound protein, 0.16 pound fat, and 1,120 calories. Expended for beef sirloin at 20 cents per pound it will furnish 0.5 pound total food matter, containing 0.08 pound protein, 0.09 pound fat, and 520 calories. If wheat bread is purchased at 5 cents per pound, 10 cents will pay for 2 pounds of total food material containing 0.18 pound protein, 0.03 pound of fat, 1.06 pounds carbohydrates, and 2,430 calories.

In many of the dietary studies made in the United States, data were recorded of the cost of different foods and the relative amount of nutritive material contributed by each in proportion to the total cost. Compared with other foods at the usual prices, eggs at 12 cents per dozen were found to be a cheap source of nutrients; at 16 cents per dozen, they were fairly expensive; and at 25 cents per dozen and over, they were very expensive. This point needs some further discussion, since the value of eggs can not fairly be estimated solely on the basis of the amount of nutrients furnished. Eggs are also valuable for giving variety to the diet and for furnishing a light, easily digested, nitrogenous food, especially suitable for breakfast or other light meal, an important item for those of sedentary habits.

Many families of moderate means make a practice of buying fresh meat for but one meal a day—i. e., dinner, using for breakfast either bacon, dried beef, codfish, or left-over meats, etc., and for lunch or supper, bread and butter and the cold meat and other foods remaining from the other two meals, with perhaps the addition of cake and fresh or preserved fruit. It is the thrifty housekeeper, who uses all her material as economically as possible in some such way, who is likely to fall into the error of excluding eggs at higher prices almost entirely from her food supply. If her economy was directed principally to restricting the use of eggs in the making of rich dessert dishes, cake, and pastry, one might not only refrain from criticising but welcome the circumstances which necessitated the making of simple and therefore more wholesome desserts. But usually the housekeeper economizes by the more obvious method of omitting to serve them as a meat substitute.

The statement so frequently made by housekeepers that eggs at 25 cents per dozen are cheaper than meat is true in one sense. Not, of course, with reference to the total amount of nutrients obtained for the money expended, but because a smaller amount of money is needed to furnish the meal. That is to say, whereas at least 1¼ pounds of beefsteak, costing 25 cents, at 20 cents per pound, would be necessary to serve five adults; in many families five eggs, costing 10 cents, at 25 cents per dozen, would serve the same number and probably satisfy them equally well. If the appetites of the family are such as to demand two eggs per person, doubling the cost, it is still 20 per cent less than the steak. Many persons eat more than two eggs at a meal, but the average number per person it is believed does not generally exceed two in most families. A hotel chef is authority for the statement that at least one-half the orders he receives are for one egg. Frequently when omelets, soufflés, creamed eggs, and other similar dishes, are served in place of fried, poached, or boiled eggs or meat, less than one egg per person is used.

These statements must not be understood as advocating a free use of eggs at any price, but merely as pointing out that even at the higher prices the occasional use of eggs in place of meat need not be regarded as a luxury. This is illustrated by observations made by Miss Bevier and Miss Sprague[1] at Lake Erie College, Ohio, during a dietary study of some 115 women, most of them students. It was found that the amount and cost of certain foods required for a single meal, when any one of them was served, was as follows:

Comparative amount and cost of certain foods required, per meal, by women students' club.

	Amount required.	Price per pound.	Total cost per meal.
	Pounds.	*Cents.*	
Beef steak	36	17	$6.12
Mutton chops	45	14	6.30
Hamburg steak	24	12½	3.00
Sausage	30	12	3.60
Bacon	12	9	1.08
Dried beef	4	23	a .92
Eggs	b 15	c 14½	2.20
Do	b 15	d 16½	2.50

a Milk, butter, and flour required for the dried beef, when creamed, would increase the cost somewhat.

b 15 pounds = 10 dozen eggs.   c Or 22 cents per dozen.   d Or 25 cents per dozen.

At the price at which board was furnished, steaks and chops were too expensive for use as breakfast dishes. Bacon or dried beef was considered cheap. Hamburg steak and sausage were regarded as practicable and were occasionally used. When the investigation was

[1] U. S. Dept. Agr., Office of Experiment Stations Bul. 91, and unpublished data furnished by Miss Sprague.

undertaken, the opinion was commonly held that eggs at 22 cents per dozen were expensive, and at 25 cents per dozen so dear that they could not be used, yet it will be seen by reference to the above table that at both prices the amount of eggs actually required to satisfy the members of the club cost less than any of the foods except bacon and dried beef. Observations showed that many of the students did not care for Hamburg steak or sausage and would eat eggs. If any boiled eggs were left, they could be used for garnishing salads or in other ways and therefore need not be wasted, while it was difficult to utilize the remnants of Hamburg steak or sausage in such a way that they were relished. It appears, therefore, that both as regards economy and palatability, the use of eggs in this case as a breakfast food was warranted.

In the instance cited, it is known that 10 dozen eggs, 30 pounds of sausage, 24 pounds of Hamburg steak, 12 pounds of bacon, and the amounts of the other foods mentioned in the table, were not equivalent as regards the quantity of nutrients furnished, although any of the foods could be used as a breakfast dish in the quantity mentioned and give satisfaction to the club. It must be remembered, however, that other foods were served with the meat or eggs, and that the total amount of nutrients consumed at the meal may not have varied greatly from day to day although the menu was quite different. Furthermore, physiologists believe that the quantities eaten each day need not conform exactly to the accepted dietary standard, but rather that the daily average throughout a considerable period must not vary very greatly from it. A deficiency on one day may be easily made good by an abundance the next. When, as was the case at Lake Erie College, each meal is abundant, the average daily diet corresponds with reasonable closeness to the commonly accepted dietary standard, and the persons consuming it have every appearance of being properly nourished, such substitutions of foods of unlike nutritive value seem justifiable on theoretical as well as on practical grounds. It hardly needs to be said that the instance cited is in accord with the ordinary household practice.

Eggs and the foods into which they enter are favorite articles of diet with very many, if not most, families, and in this as in other cases the income and the need for economy must determine how far and in what way they are to be used when they are high in price. Judged by their composition and digestibility, eggs are worthy of the high opinion in which they are usually held. Furthermore, they are generally relished. Although the physiological reason is perhaps difficult to find, it is generally conceded that the attractiveness and palatability of any food must not be forgotten in considering its true nutritive value. Refinement in matters of diet should keep pace with growth in general culture, and foods which please the esthetic sense as well as satisfy the hunger are certainly to be preferred to those which serve the latter purpose only, if they can be provided with the income at one's command.

MARKETING AND PRESERVING EGGS.

In earlier times eggs, if sold at all, were marketed near the place where they were produced. Many are still sold in local markets; but with improved methods of transportation the market has been extended and large quantities of eggs are shipped from this country and Canada not only to distant points in America, but to England and more distant countries. For shipping long distances there are special egg cases, and the shipper should select the kind which is preferred in the market which he desires to reach.

The shells of new-laid eggs should be wiped clean, if necessary, and the eggs graded as regards size. In some markets brown eggs are preferred to white. It is stated that in the Boston market brown-shelled eggs, such as are laid by Partridge Cochins, Dark Brahmas, Barred Plymouth Rocks, etc., sell at from 2 to 5 cents per dozen more than white-shelled eggs, such as are laid by Brown Leghorns, Buff Leghorns, and White and Black Minorcas. In the New York market, on the other hand, white-shelled eggs bring the higher price. That the color of the shell has no relation to the food value, as shown by analysis, is pointed out on another page (p. 13).

Eggs which are to be shipped, whether with or without a special attempt at preservation, should be perfectly fresh, and should never be packed in any material which has a disagreeable odor. Musty straw or bran will injure the flavor and keeping qualities of eggs packed in it. When shipped, eggs should not be placed near anything which has a disagreeable or strong odor. Keeping eggs near a cargo of apples during transportation has been known to injure their flavor and also their market value. As previously noted, micro-organisms may enter the egg through the minute pores in the shell and set up fermentation which ruins the egg. In other words, it becomes rotten. The normal eggshell has a natural surface coating of mucilaginous matter, which hinders the entrance of these harmful organisms for a considerable time. If this coating is removed or softened by washing or otherwise, the keeping quality of the egg is much diminished. If the process of hatching has begun, the flavor of the egg is also injured.

There are many ways of testing the freshness of eggs which are more or less satisfactory. "Candling," as it is called, is one of the methods most commonly followed. The eggs are held up in a suitable device against a light. The fresh egg appears unclouded and almost translucent; if incubation has begun, a dark spot is visible which increases in size according to the length of time incubation has continued. A rotten egg appears dark colored. Egg dealers become very expert in judging eggs by testing them by this and other methods.

The age of eggs may be approximately judged by taking advantage of the fact that as they grow old their density decreases through evaporation of moisture. According to Siebel a new-laid egg placed in a vessel of brine made in the proportion of 2 ounces of salt to 1 pint of water, will at once sink to the bottom. An egg 1 day old will sink below the surface, but not to the bottom, while one 3 days old will swim just immersed in the liquid. If more than 3 days old, the egg will float on the surface, the amount of shell exposed increasing with age; and if two weeks old, only a little of the shell will dip in the liquid.

The New York State Experiment Station studied the changes in the specific gravity of the eggs on keeping and found that on an average fresh eggs had a specific gravity of 1.090; after they were 10 days old, of 1.072; after 20 days, of 1.053, and after 30 days, of 1.035. The test was not continued further. The changes in specific gravity correspond to the changes in water content. When eggs are kept they continually lose water by evaporation through the pores in the shell. After 10 days the average loss was found to be 1.60 per cent of the total water present in the egg when perfectly fresh; after 20 days, 3.16 per cent, and after 30 days, 5 per cent. The average temperature of the room where the eggs were kept was 63.8° F. The evaporation was found to increase somewhat with increased temperature. None of the eggs used in the 30-day test spoiled.

Fresh eggs are preserved in a number of ways which may, for convenience, be grouped under two general classes: (1) Use of low temperature, i. e., cold storage; and (2) excluding the air by coating, covering, or immersing the eggs, some material or solution being used which may or may not be a germicide. The two methods are often combined. The first method owes its value to the fact that micro-organisms, like larger forms of plant life, will not grow below a certain temperature, the necessary degree of cold varying with the species. So far as experiment shows, it is impossible to kill these minute plants, popularly called " bacteria " or " germs," by any degree of cold; and so, very low temperature is unnecessary for preserving eggs, even if it were not undesirable for other reasons, such as injury by freezing and increased cost. According to a recent report of the Canadian commission of agriculture and dairying:

When fresh-laid eggs are put into cold storage with a sweet, pure atmosphere at a temperature of 34° F., very little, if any, change takes place in their quality. The egg cases should be fairly close to prevent circulation of air through them, which would cause evaporation of the egg contents.

Eggs should be carried on the cars and on the steamships [at a temperature of] from 42° to 38°. When cases containing eggs are removed from the cold-storage chamber, they should not be opened at once in an atmosphere where the temperature is warm. They should be left for two days unopened, so that the eggs may become gradually warmed to the temperature of the air in the room where they have been deposited, otherwise a condensation of moisture from the atmosphere will appear on the shell and give them the appearance of sweating. This so-called "sweating" is not an exudation through the shell of the egg, and can be entirely prevented in the manner indicated.

It is stated by Siebel that in practice in this country 32° to 33° F. is regarded as the best temperature for storing eggs, although some American packers prefer 31° to 34°, while English writers recommend a temperature of 40° to 45° as being equally satisfactory. The amount of moisture in the air in the cold-storage chamber has without doubt an important bearing on this point. Eggs are generally placed in cold storage in April and the early part of May. If placed in storage later than this time they do not keep well. They are seldom kept in storage longer than a year. Eggs which have been stored at a temperature of 30° must be used soon after removal from storage, while those stored at 35° to 40° will keep for a considerable time after removal from storage, and are said to have the flavor of fresh eggs. The author cited states that eggs for market, especially those designed for cold storage, should not be washed. Stored eggs should be turned at least twice a week, to prevent the yolk from adhering to the shell.

Eggs are sometimes removed from the shells and stored in bulk, usually on a commercial scale, in cans containing about 50 pounds each. The temperature recommended is about 30° F., or a little below freezing, and it is said they will keep any desired length of time. They must be used soon after they have been removed from storage and have been thawed.

The substances suggested and the methods tried for excluding air conveying micro-organisms to the egg, and for killing those already present, are very numerous. An old domestic method is to pack the eggs in oats or bran. Another, which has always had many advocates, consists in covering the eggs with limewater which may or may not contain salt. The results obtained by such methods are not by any means uniform. Sometimes the eggs remain fresh and of good flavor, and at other times they spoil. Recently, in Germany, twenty methods of preserving eggs were tested. The eggs were kept for eight months with the following results: Those preserved in salt water, i. e., brine, were all bad, not rotten, but unpalatable, the salt having penetrated the eggs. Of the eggs preserved by wrapping in paper, 80 per cent were bad; the same proportion of those preserved in a solution of salicylic acid and glycerin were unfit for use. Seventy per cent of the eggs rubbed with salt were bad, and the same proportion of those preserved by packing in bran, or covered with paraffin or varnished with a solution of glycerin and salycilic acid. Of the eggs sterilized by placing in boiling water for 12 to 15 seconds, 50 per cent were bad. One-half of those treated with a solution of alum or put in a solution of salicylic acid were also bad. Forty per cent of the eggs varnished with water glass, collodion, or shellac were spoiled. Twenty per cent of the eggs packed in peat dust were unfit for use, the same percentage of those preserved in wood ashes, or treated with a solution of boric acid and water glass, or with a solution of permanganate of potash were also bad. Some of the eggs were varnished with vaseline; these were all good, as were those preserved in limewater or in a solution of water glass. Of the last three methods, preservation in a solution of water glass is especially recommended, since varnishing the eggs with vaseline is time consuming, and treatment with limewater sometimes communicates to the eggs a disagreeable odor and taste.

Many of these methods have been tested at the agricultural experiment stations in this and other countries. The Canada Station found that infertile eggs kept much better than fertile eggs when packed in bran. In view of the fact that preservation in brine has been said to injure the eggs by giving them an unpleasant, salty taste, experiments were recently made at Berlin University to learn the proportion of salt which entered the eggs when placed in brine of varying strength. It was found by the investigator that with a saturated or half-saturated solution, the salt entered the eggs at first very quickly, and later much more slowly. After remaining 4 days in the saturated solution, an egg contained as much salt as one which remained 4 to 6 weeks in a 1 to 3 per cent solution. If kept in the saturated solution 4 weeks, 1.1 per cent salt was found in the yolk and 1.5 per cent in the white of the eggs. None of the eggs tested were spoiled. When a 1 to 5 per cent solution was used, the eggs kept well for 4 weeks and did not have a salty flavor. These instances are sufficient to show that any given method will give different results in different hands, and this is not surprising, since the eggs used are not always uniformly fresh, nor is it at all certain that other experimental conditions are uniform.

In the last two or three years the method of preserving eggs with a solution of water glass has been often tested both in a practical way and in laboratories. The North Dakota Experiment Station has been especially interested in the problem. In these experiments a 10 per cent solution of water glass preserved eggs so effectually that "at the end of $3\frac{1}{2}$ months eggs that were preserved the first part of August still appeared to be perfectly fresh. In most packed eggs, after a little time, the yolk settles to one side, and the egg is then inferior in quality. In eggs preserved for $3\frac{1}{2}$ months in water glass, the yolk retained its normal position in the egg, and in taste they were not to be distinguished from fresh store eggs. Again, most packed eggs will not beat up well for cake making or frosting, while eggs from a water-glass solution seemed quite equal to the average fresh eggs of the market."

Water glass or soluble glass is the popular name for potassium silicate or for sodium silicate, the commercial article often being a mixture of the two. The commercial water glass is used for preserving eggs, as it is much cheaper than the chemically pure article which is required for many scientific purposes. Water glass is commonly sold in two forms, a sirup-thick liquid, of about the consistency of molasses, and a powder. The thick sirup, the form perhaps most usually seen, is sometimes sold wholesale as low as 1¾ cents per pound in carboy lots. The retail price varies, though 10 cents per pound, according to the North Dakota Experiment Station, seems to be the price commonly asked. According to the results obtained at this station a solution of the desired strength for preserving eggs may be made by dissolving 1 part of the sirup-thick water glass in 10 parts, by measure, of water. If the water glass powder is used less is required for a given quantity of water. Much of the water glass offered for sale is very alkaline. Such material should not be used, as the eggs preserved in it will not keep well. Only pure water should be used in making the solution, and it is best to boil it and cool it before mixing with the water glass. The solution should be carefully poured over the eggs packed in a suitable vessel, which must be clean and sweet, and if wooden kegs or barrels are used they should be thoroughly scalded before packing the eggs in them. The packed eggs should be stored in a cool place. If they are placed where it is too warm silicate deposits on the shell and the eggs do not keep well. The North Dakota Experiment Station found it best not to wash the eggs before packing, as this removes the natural mucilaginous coating on the outside of the shell. The station states that 1 gallon of the solution is sufficient for 50 dozen eggs if they are properly packed.

It is, perhaps, too much to expect that eggs packed in any way will be just as satisfactory for table use as the fresh article. The opinion seems to be, however, that those preserved with water glass are superior to most of those preserved otherwise. The shells of eggs preserved in water glass are apt to crack in boiling. It is stated that this may be prevented by puncturing the blunt end of the egg with a pin before putting it into the water.

In the East Indian Archipelago salted ducks' eggs are an article of diet. The new-laid eggs are packed for 2 or 3 weeks in a mixture of clay, brick dust, and salt. They are eaten hard-boiled. It is said that in this region and in India turtle eggs are also preserved in salt. These products, while unusual, do not necessarily suggest an unpleasant article of diet. The same can hardly be said of a Chinese product which has often been described. Ducks' eggs are buried in the ground for 10 or 12 months and undergo a peculiar fermentation. The hydrogen sulphid formed breaks the shell and escapes while the egg becomes hard in texture. It is said that the final product does not possess a disagreeable odor or taste. Eggs treated in this or some similar way are on sale in the Chinese quarter of San Francisco, and very likely in other American cities. A sample recently examined had the appearance of an egg covered with dark-colored clay or mud.

SELLING EGGS BY WEIGHT.

Since eggs vary more or less in size it has been proposed that they should be sold by weight rather than by the dozen, which is the usual custom in this country. The North Carolina Experiment Station, in investigating this point, recorded the weight of eggs per dozen and the number produced during six months by pullets and old hens of a number of well-known breeds and by ducks. Generally speaking, larger eggs were laid by hens than by pullets of the same breed. The eggs laid by Pekin ducks (old and young) averaged 35.6 ounces per dozen, and were heavier than those laid by any breed of hens. Of the different breeds of hens tested the largest eggs weighed 28 ounces per dozen, and were laid by Light Brahmas. The Black Langshan and Barred Plymouth Rock hens' eggs weighed a little over 26 ounces per dozen, while those laid by Single Comb Brown Leghorns, late hatched Plymouth Rock, White Wyandotte, and Buff Cochin hens ranged from 21.7 to 23.7 ounces per dozen.

Of the pullets, the heaviest eggs (weighing 26.5 ounces per dozen) were laid by the Black Minorcas, the lightest by the Single Comb Brown Leghorns and Silver-Laced Wyandottes. These weighed 17.5 and 22.1 ounces per dozen, respectively. The Barred Plymouth Rock, White Plymouth Rock, White Wyandotte, Black Langshan, and Buff Cochin pullets' eggs all weighed not far from 24 ounces per dozen. As will be seen, the variation in the weight of the eggs was considerable. In tests carried on at the Maine Experiment Station it was noticed that eggs from hens that laid the greatest number were on an average smaller in size than those from hens producing fewer eggs. The percentage of fertility was also less in the former than in the latter.

In the North Carolina test all of the eggs, regardless of size, had a local market value of 13½ cents per dozen at the time of the investigation. If a dozen Single Comb Brown Leghorn pullets' eggs weighing 17½ ounces were worth 13½ cents per dozen, or 12 cents per pound, the eggs of the other breeds would be actually worth from 16.3 cents for the Single Comb Brown Leghorn hens to 21.6 cents per dozen for the Light Brahma hens, or from 20.7 to 60 per cent in excess of their market value. The eggs of the Pekin ducks would be worth 26.7 cents, or 97.8 per cent above their market value. On the basis of the results obtained, the station advocates selling eggs by the pound instead of by the dozen. It is said that the egg packers and dealers maintain that this method would increase the cost of the eggs, owing to the extra handling necessary and the consequent breakage. An apparent objection to selling eggs by weight is that they are not generally used in the household in this way. Most recipes call for eggs by number and not by weight. There is no question that weighing the eggs would be more accurate, and recipes are occasionally met with in which this method is followed.

DESICCATED EGGS, EGG POWDERS, AND EGG SUBSTITUTES.

Different methods of evaporating or desiccating eggs have been proposed and several products which claim to be prepared in this way are now on the market. It is said that the egg is dried in or out of a vacuum, usually by a gentle heat or by currents of air. When placed on the market the dried egg is usually ground. Sometimes salt, sugar, or both have been used as preservatives. As will be seen by reference to the table of composition (p. 12), such material is merely egg from which the bulk of the water has been removed. If the process of manufacture is such that the resulting product is palatable and keeps well, the value of evaporated eggs under many circumstances is evident.

This material is used by bakers to some extent as being cheaper when fresh eggs are high in price. It is also used in provisioning camps and expeditions, since desiccated foods have the advantage of a higher nutritive value in proportion to their bulk than the same materials when fresh. Fresh eggs contain about 25 per cent of dry matter. If all the water is removed in preparing evaporated eggs, 1 pound will furnish nutritive material equivalent to about 4 pounds of fresh eggs. One of the commercial egg products recently tested appeared to be dried egg coarsely ground. For use it was thoroughly mixed with a small quantity of water. The mixture could then be fried or made into an omelet, etc., and was found to be very palatable, closely resembling in taste the same dishes made from fresh eggs.

An egg substitute has been manufactured from skim milk. It is said to contain the casein and albumen of the milk mixed with a little flour, and is put up in the form of a paste or powder. Such material is evidently rich in protein and, according to reports apparently reliable, is used in considerable quantities by bakers and confectioners in place of fresh eggs.

Egg substitutes have been devised which consist of mixtures of animal or vegetable fats, albumen, starch or flour, coloring matter, and some leavening powder in addition to the mineral matters similar to those found in the egg. Such products are designed to resemble eggs in composition.

Other egg substitutes have been marketed which contain little or no albumen, but apparently consist quite largely of starch, colored more or less with some yellow substance. These goods are specially recommended for making custards and puddings similar in appearance to those in which fresh eggs are used. There is no reason to suppose that such products can not be made so that they will be perfectly wholesome. The fact must not be overlooked that in the diet they can not replace fresh eggs, since they do not contain much nitrogenous matter or fat. As recently pointed out in one of the medical journals, this may be an important matter if such an egg substitute is used in the diet of invalids, especially if the composition of the egg substitute is not known, and it is employed with the belief that, like eggs, it contains an abundance of protein.

POSSIBLE DANGER FROM EATING EGGS.

Occasionally a person is found who is habitually made ill by eating eggs, just as there are those who can not eat strawberries or other foods without distress. Such cases are due to some personal idiosyncrasy, showing that in reality "one man's meat is another man's poison." A satisfactory explanation of such idiosyncrasy seems to be lacking.

Overindulgence in eggs, as is the case with other foods, may induce indigestion or other bad effects. Furthermore, under certain conditions eggs may be the cause of illness by communicating some bacterial disease or some parasite. It is possible for an egg to become infected with micro-organisms, either before it is laid or after. The shell is porous, and offers no greater resistance to micro-organisms which cause disease than it does to those which cause the egg to spoil or rot. When the infected egg is eaten raw the micro-organisms, if present, are communicated to man and may cause disease. If an egg remains in a dirty nest, defiled with the micro-organisms which cause typhoid fever, carried there on the hen's feet or feathers, it is not strange if some of these bacteria occasionally penetrate the shell and the egg thus becomes a possible source of infection. Perhaps one of the most common troubles due to bacterial infection of eggs is the more or less serious illness sometimes caused by eating those which are "stale." This often resembles ptomaine poisoning, which is caused, not by micro-organisms themselves, but by the poisonous products which they elaborate from materials on which they grow.

Occasionally the eggs of worms, etc., have been found inside hens' eggs, as indeed have grains, seeds, etc. Such bodies were doubtless accidentally occluded while the white and shell were being added to the yolk in the egg gland of the fowl.

Judged by the comparatively small number of cases of infection or poisoning due to eggs reported in medical literature, the danger of disease from this source is not very great. However, in view of its possibility, it is best to keep eggs as clean as possible and thus endeavor to prevent infection. Clean poultry houses, poultry runs, and nests are important, and eggs should always be stored and marketed under sanitary conditions. The subject of handling food in a cleanly manner is too seldom thought of, and what is said of eggs in this connection applies to many other foods with even more force.

IMPORTANCE OF THE EGG INDUSTRY.

The egg industry is of considerable commercial importance. The total number of eggs produced in the United States in 1890 was estimated to be 820,000,000 dozen, and these figures are quite often said to be too low. The United States formerly imported a large number of eggs and exported very few. The ratio has changed within the last ten years, and now the exports largely exceed the imports.

Growth of the egg industry.—In 1890 the total number of eggs exported was in round numbers 381,000 dozen, worth $59,000; in 1899, 3,694,000 dozen, worth $641,000. In 1890 this country imported 15,000,000 dozen, which were valued at $2,000,000, and in 1899 only 225,000 dozen, valued at $21,000.

Taking into account the five years up to and including 1898, 61 per cent of the exported eggs were sent to Cuba, 20 per cent to Canada, and 11 per cent to Great Britain, while the remainder was distributed among many other countries. During the same period, 96 per cent of the eggs imported came from Canada, 3 per cent from China, and the remainder from various other countries.

These statistics of the egg trade are of interest, since they show the great growth of the poultry industry, and indicate what it may become in the future. Some of the developments may be fairly attributed to the work of the Government and the agricultural experiment sta tions. For many years a considerable number of the stations, especially those in Alabama, California, Indiana, Kentucky, Louisiana, Maine, Massachusetts, Michigan, New York, North Carolina, North Dakota, Oklahoma, Oregon, Rhode Island, South Carolina, Utah, and West Virginia, have been experimenting upon methods of feeding and caring for poultry, the comparative value of different breeds, the possibility of increasing egg production by proper feeding and the selection of laying stock, and similar problems. The station bulletins reporting the investigations have been circulated widely. These investigations are being continued and promise to be even more valuable in their results in the future than in the past. The Department of Agriculture has done much to encourage the poultry industry by collecting and distributing information,[1] and in other ways.

Poultry raising is often carried on in conjunction with general farm ing, and may be profitably developed along such lines. When it is fol lowed as an independent enterprise, its possibilities are also great. There is always a market for poultry and eggs for food, while the raising of fancy stock for breeding purposes is frequently worth consideration.

---

[1] Farmers' Bulletins 41, 51, and 64 of the Department are devoted exclusively to poultry topics. A number of Farmers' Bulletins of the series entitled "Experiment Station Work" contain short articles on poultry, poultry feeding, or similar topics. A bibliography of poultry literature has been published by the Department Library (Bul. 18). Bulletin 5 of the Division of Publications contains a list of references to articles on eggs and poultry in the Department publications. A number of the publications of the Bureau of Animal Industry contain articles on poultry diseases, egg production, and other topics, while many of the publications of the Section of Foreign Markets give statistics of the poultry and egg industry.

FARMERS' BULLETINS.

The following is a list of the Farmers' Bulletins available for distribution, showing the number, title, and size in pages of each. Copies will be sent to any address on application to Senators, Representatives, and Delegates in Congress, or to the Secretary of Agriculture, Washington, D. C.:

16. Leguminous Plants. Pp. 24.
19. Important Insecticides. Pp. 32.
21. Barnyard Manure. Pp. 32.
22. The Feeding of Farm Animals. Pp. 32.
23. Foods: Nutritive Value and Cost. Pp. 32.
24. Hog Cholera and Swine Plague. Pp. 16.
25. Peanuts: Culture and Uses. Pp. 24.
26. Sweet Potatoes: Culture and Uses. Pp. 30.
27. Flax for Seed and Fiber. Pp. 16.
28. Weeds: And How to Kill Them. Pp. 32.
29. Souring and Other Changes in Milk. Pp. 23.
30. Grape Diseases on the Pacific Coast. Pp. 15.
31. Alfalfa, or Lucern. Pp. 24.
32. Silos and Silage. Pp. 32.
33. Peach Growing for Market. Pp. 24.
34. Meats: Composition and Cooking. Pp. 29.
35. Potato Culture. Pp. 24.
36. Cotton Seed and Its Products. Pp. 16.
37. Kafir Corn: Culture and Uses. Pp. 12.
38. Spraying for Fruit Diseases. Pp. 12.
39. Onion Culture. Pp. 31.
40. Farm Drainage. Pp. 24.
41. Fowls: Care and Feeding. Pp. 24.
42. Facts About Milk. .Pp. 29.
43. Sewage Disposal on the Farm. Pp. 20.
44. Commercial Fertilizers. Pp. 24.
45. Insects Injurious to Stored Grain. Pp. 24.
46. Irrigation in Humid Climates. Pp. 27.
47. Insects Affecting the Cotton Plant. Pp. 32.
48. The Manuring of Cotton. Pp. 16.
49. Sheep Feeding. Pp. 24.
50. Sorghum as a Forage Crop. Pp. 20.
51. Standard Varieties of Chickens. Pp. 48.
52. The Sugar Beet. Pp. 48.
53. How to Grow Mushrooms. Pp. 20.
54. Some Common Birds. Pp. 40.
55. The Dairy Herd. Pp. 24.
56. Experiment Station Work—I. Pp. 31.
57. Butter Making on the Farm. Pp. 16.
58. The Soy Bean as a Forage Crop. Pp. 24.
59. Bee Keeping. Pp. 32.
60. Methods of Curing Tobacco. Pp. 16.
61. Asparagus Culture. Pp. 40.
62. Marketing Farm Produce. Pp. 28.
63. Care of Milk on the Farm. Pp. 40.
64. Ducks and Geese. Pp. 48.
65. Experiment Station Work—II. Pp. 32.
66. Meadows and Pastures. Pp. 28.
67. Forestry for Farmers. Pp. 48.
68. The Black Rot of the Cabbage. Pp. 22.
69. Experiment Station Work—III. Pp. 32.
70. Insect Enemies of the Grape. Pp. 23.
71. Essentials in Beef Production. Pp. 24.
72. Cattle Ranges of the Southwest. Pp. 32.
73. Experiment Station Work—IV. Pp. 32.
74. Milk as Food. Pp. 39.
75. The Grain Smuts. Pp. 20.
76. Tomato Growing. Pp. 30.

77. The Liming of Soils. Pp. 19.
78. Experiment Station Work—V. Pp. 32.
79. Experiment Station Work—VI. Pp. 28.
80. The Peach Twig-borer. Pp. 16.
81. Corn Culture in the South. Pp. 24.
82. The Culture of Tobacco. Pp. 24.
83. Tobacco Soils. Pp. 23.
84. Experiment Station Work—VII. Pp. 32.
85. Fish as Food. Pp. 30.
86. Thirty Poisonous Plants. Pp. 32.
87. Experiment Station Work—VIII. Pp. 32.
88. Alkali Lands. Pp. 23.
89. Cowpeas. Pp. 16.
90. The Manufacture of Sorghum Sirup. Pp. 32.
91. Potato Diseases and Their Treatment. Pp. 12.
92. Experiment Station Work—IX. Pp. 30.
93. Sugar as Food. Pp. 27.
94. The Vegetable Garden. Pp. 24.
95. Good Roads for Farmers. Pp. 47.
96. Raising Sheep for Mutton. Pp. 48.
97. Experiment Station Work—X. Pp. 32.
98. Suggestions to Southern Farmers. Pp. 48.
99. Three Insect Enemies of Shade Trees. Pp. 30.
100. Hog Raising in the South. Pp. 40.
101. Millets. Pp. 28.
102. Southern Forage Plants. Pp. 48.
103. Experiment Station Work—XI. Pp. 32.
104. Notes on Frost. Pp. 24.
105. Experiment Station Work—XII. Pp. 32.
.106. Breeds of Dairy Cattle. Pp. 48.
107. Experiment Station Work—XIII. Pp. 32.
108. Saltbushes. Pp. 20.
109. Farmers' Reading Courses. Pp. 20.
110. Rice Culture in the United States. Pp. 28.
111. The Farmer's Interest in Good Seed. Pp. 24.
112. Bread and Bread Making. Pp. 39.
113. The Apple and How to Grow It. Pp. 32.
114. Experiment Station Work—XIV. Pp. 28.
115. Hop Culture in California. Pp. 27.
116. Irrigation in Fruit Growing. Pp. 48.
117. Sheep, Hogs, and Horses in the Northwest. Pp. 28.
118. Grape Growing in the South. Pp. 32.
119. Experiment Station Work—XV. Pp. 31.
120. The Principal Insects Affecting the Tobacco Plant. Pp. 32.
121. Beans, Peas, and other Legumes as Food. Pp. 32.
122. Experiment Station Work—XVI. Pp. 32.
123. Red Clover Seed: Information for Purchasers. Pp. 11.
124. Experiment Station Work—XVII. Pp. 32.
125. Protection of Food Products from Injurious Temperature. Pp. 26.
126. Practical Suggestions for Farm Buildings. (In press.)
127. Important Insecticides: Directions for Their Preparation and use.